A Gratitude Journal

FOR WOMEN

A Gratitude Journal

FOR WOMEN

Introduction

Hey! I'm Brie Resilient—the creator of your new (*and soon to be favorite*) journal.

This daily gratitude journal is an invitation for you to explore yourself in unique ways reserved only for those who put pen to paper. These lined pages are more than a place for you to write, **but a place for you to discover the good within your life.**

Gratitude helps you create the life you hold within your heart and secretly wish for each night. It's what makes life more than enough because it enables you to appreciate what you have, as well as prepare you for what you want.

Gratitude is a practice, a commitment, a daily decision to focus on the good, and the more you do it, *the better life gets.*

With so much love,

Brie Resilient

Gratitude Journal

fill in the date

08 /11 /2023

Give the world the best you have, and the best will come back to you.

MADELINE BRIDGES

TODAY I AM GRATEFUL FOR

MY INTENTION FOR TODAY IS

ex. Appreciate the little things.

your happiness matters, so don't skip this one!

ONE THING TO DO FOR MYSELF TODAY

WHAT CAN I DO TODAY TO FEEL
choose one

happy / healthy / kind / content / peaceful / patient / inspired

HOW TO USE THIS
Gratitude Journal

Write a little, or write a lot. This gratitude journal will be as unique as you are!

I COMMIT TO BEING GRATEFUL TODAY ☑

Check the box when you're done!

HOW TO CREATE TIME FOR YOUR
Gratitude Journal

1.
YOU'RE A SELF-PROFESSED CONTROL FREAK
and you like it that way.

2.
YOU'RE IN LOVE WITH YOUR PLANNER
*and live to cross off every last line on your to-do list because
you're all about that super productive life.*

3.
BUT LATELY YOU'VE BEEN EXHAUSTED
and the control that helped you succeed is now stressing you out.

4.
SOMETHING'S OUT OF BALANCE *friends? family? love life?*

5.
RARELY ARE YOU ENJOYING TIME FOR YOURSELF

6.
YOU HAVEN'T JOURNALED IN MONTHS

we've all been there ### 7.
YOU'RE TOO BUSY,
and miss making you a priority

I'm Brie Resilient...

I've been where you are. It took years for me to learn how to integrate balance, joy and positivity into my life—no matter how crazy life got.

Deciding that my happiness mattered (*and yours does too*), I began to research, test and tweak different ways to jumpstart my days with a shot of joy.

I soon learned that the secret solution was how I used my mornings, and it's this that I want to share with you!

Ready to know the secret?

(Turn to page 106.)

JOURNALING IS LIKE WHISPERING TO ONE'S SELF AND LISTENING AT THE SAME TIME.

MINA MURRAY

Give the world the best you have, and the best will come back to you.

MADELINE BRIDGES

TODAY I AM GRATEFUL FOR

_____

_____

_____

_____

_____

_____

_____

_____

_____

_____

MY INTENTION FOR TODAY IS

_____

_____

_____

ONE THING TO DO FOR MYSELF TODAY

_____

_____

_____

WHAT CAN I DO TODAY TO FEEL

(Choose one.)

happy / healthy / kind / content / peaceful / patient / inspired

_____

_____

_____

_____

THOUGHTS

_____
_____
_____
_____
_____
_____
_____
_____
_____
_____
_____
_____
_____
_____
_____
_____
_____
_____
_____
_____
_____
_____
_____
_____
_____
_____
_____
_____
_____
_____

I COMMIT TO BEING GRATEFUL TODAY ☐

Talents are best nurtured in solitude; character is best formed in the stormy billows of the world.

GOETHE

TODAY I AM GRATEFUL FOR

MY INTENTION FOR TODAY IS

ONE THING TO DO FOR MYSELF TODAY

WHAT CAN I DO TODAY TO FEEL

(Choose one.)

happy   /   healthy   /   kind   /   content   /   peaceful   /   patient   /   inspired

THOUGHTS

Those who don't know how to weep with their whole heart don't know how to laugh either.

GOLDA MEIR

TODAY I AM GRATEFUL FOR

_____

_____

_____

_____

_____

_____

_____

_____

_____

_____

_____

MY INTENTION FOR TODAY IS

_____

_____

_____

ONE THING TO DO FOR MYSELF TODAY

_____

_____

WHAT CAN I DO TODAY TO FEEL

(Choose one.)

happy / healthy / kind / content / peaceful / patient / inspired

_____

_____

_____

THOUGHTS

I COMMIT TO BEING GRATEFUL TODAY ☐

And now these 3 remain; faith, hope and love. But the greatest of these is love.

1 CORINTHIANS 13: 13

TODAY I AM GRATEFUL FOR

MY INTENTION FOR TODAY IS

ONE THING TO DO FOR MYSELF TODAY

WHAT CAN I DO TODAY TO FEEL

(Choose one.)

happy   /   healthy   /   kind   /   content   /   peaceful   /   patient   /   inspired

THOUGHTS

_____
_____
_____
_____
_____
_____
_____
_____
_____
_____
_____
_____
_____
_____
_____
_____
_____
_____
_____
_____
_____
_____
_____
_____
_____
_____
_____
_____
_____

I COMMIT TO BEING GRATEFUL TODAY ☐

There are many ways to measure success; not the least of which is the way your child describes you when talking to a friend.

ANONYMOUS

TODAY I AM GRATEFUL FOR

_____

_____

_____

_____

_____

_____

_____

_____

_____

_____

MY INTENTION FOR TODAY IS

_____

_____

_____

ONE THING TO DO FOR MYSELF TODAY

_____

_____

WHAT CAN I DO TODAY TO FEEL

(Choose one.)

happy   /   healthy   /   kind   /   content   /   peaceful   /   patient   /   inspired

_____

_____

_____

THOUGHTS

I COMMIT TO BEING GRATEFUL TODAY ☐

Happiness is the meaning and the purpose of life, the whole aim and end of human existence.

ARISTOTLE

TODAY I AM GRATEFUL FOR

_____

_____

_____

_____

_____

_____

_____

_____

_____

_____

_____

MY INTENTION FOR TODAY IS

_____

_____

_____

ONE THING TO DO FOR MYSELF TODAY

_____

_____

WHAT CAN I DO TODAY TO FEEL

(Choose one.)

happy / healthy / kind / content / peaceful / patient / inspired

_____

_____

_____

THOUGHTS

Friends are family you choose for yourself.

JANE ADAMS

TODAY I AM GRATEFUL FOR

_____

_____

_____

_____

_____

_____

_____

_____

_____

_____

_____

MY INTENTION FOR TODAY IS

_____

_____

_____

ONE THING TO DO FOR MYSELF TODAY

_____

_____

WHAT CAN I DO TODAY TO FEEL

(Choose one.)

happy   /   healthy   /   kind   /   content   /   peaceful   /   patient   /   inspired

_____

_____

_____

THOUGHTS

_____

_____

_____

_____

_____

_____

_____

_____

_____

_____

_____

_____

_____

_____

_____

_____

_____

_____

_____

_____

_____

_____

_____

_____

_____

_____

_____

_____

_____

_____

I COMMIT TO BEING GRATEFUL TODAY ☐

An early morning walk is a blessing for the whole day.

HENRY DAVID THOREAU

TODAY I AM GRATEFUL FOR

_____

_____

_____

_____

_____

_____

_____

_____

_____

_____

MY INTENTION FOR TODAY IS

_____

_____

_____

_____

ONE THING TO DO FOR MYSELF TODAY

_____

_____

_____

WHAT CAN I DO TODAY TO FEEL

(Choose one.)

happy   /   healthy   /   kind   /   content   /   peaceful   /   patient   /   inspired

_____

_____

_____

_____

THOUGHTS

_____
_____
_____
_____
_____
_____
_____
_____
_____
_____
_____
_____
_____
_____
_____
_____
_____
_____
_____
_____
_____
_____
_____
_____
_____
_____
_____

I COMMIT TO BEING GRATEFUL TODAY ☐

Venture outside your comfort zone. The rewards are worth it.

RAPUNZEL, TANGLED

TODAY I AM GRATEFUL FOR

_____
_____
_____
_____
_____
_____
_____
_____
_____
_____
_____

MY INTENTION FOR TODAY IS

_____
_____
_____

ONE THING TO DO FOR MYSELF TODAY

_____
_____

WHAT CAN I DO TODAY TO FEEL

(Choose one.)

happy   /   healthy   /   kind   /   content   /   peaceful   /   patient   /   inspired

_____
_____
_____
_____

THOUGHTS

I COMMIT TO BEING GRATEFUL TODAY ☐

Success follows doing what you want to do. There is no other way to be successful

MALCOLM FORBES

TODAY I AM GRATEFUL FOR

_____

_____

_____

_____

_____

_____

_____

_____

_____

_____

MY INTENTION FOR TODAY IS

_____

_____

_____

ONE THING TO DO FOR MYSELF TODAY

_____

_____

WHAT CAN I DO TODAY TO FEEL

(Choose one.)

happy / healthy / kind / content / peaceful / patient / inspired

_____

_____

_____

_____

THOUGHTS

I COMMIT TO BEING GRATEFUL TODAY ☐

Parents can only give good advice or put them on the right paths, but the final forming of a person's character lies in their own hands.

ANNE FRANK

TODAY I AM GRATEFUL FOR

_____
_____
_____
_____
_____
_____
_____
_____
_____
_____
_____

MY INTENTION FOR TODAY IS

_____
_____
_____

ONE THING TO DO FOR MYSELF TODAY

_____
_____

WHAT CAN I DO TODAY TO FEEL

(Choose one.)

happy / healthy / kind / content / peaceful / patient / inspired

_____
_____
_____
_____

THOUGHTS

In the small matters, trust the mind. In the large ones, trust the heart.

SIGMUND FREUD

TODAY I AM GRATEFUL FOR

_____

_____

_____

_____

_____

_____

_____

_____

_____

_____

_____

MY INTENTION FOR TODAY IS

_____

_____

_____

_____

ONE THING TO DO FOR MYSELF TODAY

_____

_____

WHAT CAN I DO TODAY TO FEEL

(Choose one.)

happy   /   healthy   /   kind   /   content   /   peaceful   /   patient   /   inspired

_____

_____

_____

_____

THOUGHTS

To love is to receive a glimpse of heaven.

KAREN SUNDE

TODAY I AM GRATEFUL FOR

MY INTENTION FOR TODAY IS

ONE THING TO DO FOR MYSELF TODAY

WHAT CAN I DO TODAY TO FEEL

(Choose one.)

happy   /   healthy   /   kind   /   content   /   peaceful   /   patient   /   inspired

---

THOUGHTS

_____

_____

_____

_____

_____

_____

_____

_____

_____

_____

_____

_____

_____

_____

_____

_____

_____

_____

_____

_____

_____

_____

_____

_____

_____

_____

_____

I COMMIT TO BEING GRATEFUL TODAY ☐

Enjoy the little things, for one day you may look back and realize they were the big things.

ROBERT BRAULT

TODAY I AM GRATEFUL FOR

_____

_____

_____

_____

_____

_____

_____

_____

_____

_____

_____

MY INTENTION FOR TODAY IS

_____

_____

_____

_____

ONE THING TO DO FOR MYSELF TODAY

_____

_____

_____

WHAT CAN I DO TODAY TO FEEL

(Choose one.)

happy / healthy / kind / content / peaceful / patient / inspired

_____

_____

_____

_____

THOUGHTS

I COMMIT TO BEING GRATEFUL TODAY ☐

Life is either a daring adventure or nothing.

HELEN KELLER

TODAY I AM GRATEFUL FOR

MY INTENTION FOR TODAY IS

ONE THING TO DO FOR MYSELF TODAY

WHAT CAN I DO TODAY TO FEEL

(Choose one.)

happy / healthy / kind / content / peaceful / patient / inspired

---

THOUGHTS

"...The real friend... is, as it were, another self.

CICERO

TODAY I AM GRATEFUL FOR

_____

_____

_____

_____

_____

_____

_____

_____

_____

_____

_____

_____

MY INTENTION FOR TODAY IS

_____

_____

_____

_____

ONE THING TO DO FOR MYSELF TODAY

_____

_____

_____

WHAT CAN I DO TODAY TO FEEL

(Choose one.)

happy   /   healthy   /   kind   /   content   /   peaceful   /   patient   /   inspired

_____

_____

_____

_____

THOUGHTS

If people are suffering, then they must look within themselves... Happiness is not something ready-made. It comes from your own actions.

THE DALAI LAMA

TODAY I AM GRATEFUL FOR

_____

_____

_____

_____

_____

_____

_____

_____

_____

MY INTENTION FOR TODAY IS

_____

_____

_____

ONE THING TO DO FOR MYSELF TODAY

_____

_____

WHAT CAN I DO TODAY TO FEEL

(Choose one.)

happy / healthy / kind / content / peaceful / patient / inspired

_____

_____

_____

THOUGHTS

I COMMIT TO BEING GRATEFUL TODAY ☐

The greatest wealth is health.

VIRGIL

TODAY I AM GRATEFUL FOR

_____

_____

_____

_____

_____

_____

_____

_____

_____

_____

MY INTENTION FOR TODAY IS

_____

_____

_____

_____

ONE THING TO DO FOR MYSELF TODAY

_____

_____

_____

WHAT CAN I DO TODAY TO FEEL

(Choose one.)

happy / healthy / kind / content / peaceful / patient / inspired

_____

_____

_____

_____

THOUGHTS

/   /

Nothing's impossible.

ALICE IN WONDERLAND

TODAY I AM GRATEFUL FOR

_____
_____
_____
_____
_____
_____
_____
_____
_____
_____
_____

MY INTENTION FOR TODAY IS

_____
_____
_____

ONE THING TO DO FOR MYSELF TODAY

_____
_____

WHAT CAN I DO TODAY TO FEEL

(Choose one.)

happy / healthy / kind / content / peaceful / patient / inspired

_____
_____
_____

THOUGHTS

I COMMIT TO BEING GRATEFUL TODAY ☐

To find out what one is fitted to do, and to secure an opportunity to do it, is the key to happiness.

JOHN DEWEY

TODAY I AM GRATEFUL FOR

_____

_____

_____

_____

_____

_____

_____

_____

_____

_____

_____

MY INTENTION FOR TODAY IS

_____

_____

_____

ONE THING TO DO FOR MYSELF TODAY

_____

_____

WHAT CAN I DO TODAY TO FEEL

(Choose one.)

happy / healthy / kind / content / peaceful / patient / inspired

_____

_____

_____

THOUGHTS

_____

_____

_____

_____

_____

_____

_____

_____

_____

_____

_____

_____

_____

_____

_____

_____

_____

_____

_____

_____

_____

_____

_____

_____

_____

I COMMIT TO BEING GRATEFUL TODAY ☐

It is never too late to be what you might have been.

GEORGE ELIOT

TODAY I AM GRATEFUL FOR

MY INTENTION FOR TODAY IS

ONE THING TO DO FOR MYSELF TODAY

WHAT CAN I DO TODAY TO FEEL

(Choose one.)

happy   /   healthy   /   kind   /   content   /   peaceful   /   patient   /   inspired

THOUGHTS

Most folks are about as happy as they make up their minds to be.

ABRAHAM LINCOLN

TODAY I AM GRATEFUL FOR

_____

_____

_____

_____

_____

_____

_____

_____

_____

_____

_____

MY INTENTION FOR TODAY IS

_____

_____

_____

_____

ONE THING TO DO FOR MYSELF TODAY

_____

_____

WHAT CAN I DO TODAY TO FEEL

(Choose one.)

happy   /   healthy   /   kind   /   content   /   peaceful   /   patient   /   inspired

_____

_____

_____

_____

THOUGHTS

I COMMIT TO BEING GRATEFUL TODAY ☐

A goal, a love and a dream give you total control over your body and your life.

JOHN WAYNE SCHLATTER

TODAY I AM GRATEFUL FOR

_____

_____

_____

_____

_____

_____

_____

_____

_____

_____

_____

MY INTENTION FOR TODAY IS

_____

_____

_____

ONE THING TO DO FOR MYSELF TODAY

_____

_____

WHAT CAN I DO TODAY TO FEEL

(Choose one.)

happy   /   healthy   /   kind   /   content   /   peaceful   /   patient   /   inspired

_____

_____

_____

THOUGHTS

I COMMIT TO BEING GRATEFUL TODAY

Time you enjoyed wasting is not wasted time.

T. S. ELLIOT

TODAY I AM GRATEFUL FOR

_____

_____

_____

_____

_____

_____

_____

_____

_____

_____

MY INTENTION FOR TODAY IS

_____

_____

_____

ONE THING TO DO FOR MYSELF TODAY

_____

_____

WHAT CAN I DO TODAY TO FEEL

(Choose one.)

happy / healthy / kind / content / peaceful / patient / inspired

_____

_____

_____

THOUGHTS

I COMMIT TO BEING GRATEFUL TODAY ☐

Friendship is the source of the greatest pleasures, and without friends even the most agreeable pursuits become tedious.

SAINT THOMAS AQUINAS

TODAY I AM GRATEFUL FOR

MY INTENTION FOR TODAY IS

ONE THING TO DO FOR MYSELF TODAY

WHAT CAN I DO TODAY TO FEEL

(Choose one.)

happy / healthy / kind / content / peaceful / patient / inspired

THOUGHTS

I COMMIT TO BEING GRATEFUL TODAY ☐

Be a lamp to yourself. Be your own confidence. Hold to the truth within yourself, as to the only truth.

BUDDHA

TODAY I AM GRATEFUL FOR

_____

_____

_____

_____

_____

_____

_____

_____

_____

_____

_____

MY INTENTION FOR TODAY IS

_____

_____

_____

ONE THING TO DO FOR MYSELF TODAY

_____

_____

WHAT CAN I DO TODAY TO FEEL

(Choose one.)

happy / healthy / kind / content / peaceful / patient / inspired

_____

_____

_____

_____

THOUGHTS

I COMMIT TO BEING GRATEFUL TODAY ☐

Those who think they have not the time for bodily exercise will sooner or later have to find time for illness.

EDWARD STANLEY

TODAY I AM GRATEFUL FOR

_____

_____

_____

_____

_____

_____

_____

_____

_____

_____

_____

MY INTENTION FOR TODAY IS

_____

_____

_____

_____

ONE THING TO DO FOR MYSELF TODAY

_____

_____

_____

WHAT CAN I DO TODAY TO FEEL

(Choose one.)

happy / healthy / kind / content / peaceful / patient / inspired

_____

_____

_____

_____

THOUGHTS

_____

_____

_____

_____

_____

_____

_____

_____

_____

_____

_____

_____

_____

_____

_____

_____

_____

_____

_____

_____

_____

_____

_____

_____

_____

_____

_____

_____

_____

_____

I COMMIT TO BEING GRATEFUL TODAY ☐

Or fate lives within us; you only have to be brave enough to see it.

MERIDA, BRAVE

TODAY I AM GRATEFUL FOR

_____

_____

_____

_____

_____

_____

_____

_____

_____

_____

_____

MY INTENTION FOR TODAY IS

_____

_____

_____

_____

ONE THING TO DO FOR MYSELF TODAY

_____

_____

_____

WHAT CAN I DO TODAY TO FEEL

(Choose one.)

happy / healthy / kind / content / peaceful / patient / inspired

_____

_____

_____

_____

THOUGHTS

The service we render others is the rent we pay for our room on earth.

WILFRED GRENFELL

TODAY I AM GRATEFUL FOR

_____

_____

_____

_____

_____

_____

_____

_____

_____

_____

_____

_____

MY INTENTION FOR TODAY IS

_____

_____

_____

_____

ONE THING TO DO FOR MYSELF TODAY

_____

_____

WHAT CAN I DO TODAY TO FEEL

(Choose one.)

happy / healthy / kind / content / peaceful / patient / inspired

_____

_____

_____

_____

THOUGHTS

I COMMIT TO BEING GRATEFUL TODAY ☐

Think like a person of action, act like a person of thought.

HENRI BERGSON

TODAY I AM GRATEFUL FOR

_____

_____

_____

_____

_____

_____

_____

_____

_____

_____

_____

MY INTENTION FOR TODAY IS

_____

_____

_____

ONE THING TO DO FOR MYSELF TODAY

_____

_____

WHAT CAN I DO TODAY TO FEEL

(Choose one.)

happy   /   healthy   /   kind   /   content   /   peaceful   /   patient   /   inspired

_____

_____

_____

THOUGHTS

I COMMIT TO BEING GRATEFUL TODAY

Nothing which life has to offer is worth the price of worry.

NAPOLEON HILL

TODAY I AM GRATEFUL FOR

_____

_____

_____

_____

_____

_____

_____

_____

_____

_____

MY INTENTION FOR TODAY IS

_____

_____

_____

ONE THING TO DO FOR MYSELF TODAY

_____

_____

WHAT CAN I DO TODAY TO FEEL

(Choose one.)

happy   /   healthy   /   kind   /   content   /   peaceful   /   patient   /   inspired

_____

_____

_____

THOUGHTS

_____

_____

_____

_____

_____

_____

_____

_____

_____

_____

_____

_____

_____

_____

_____

_____

_____

_____

_____

_____

_____

_____

_____

_____

_____

_____

_____

I COMMIT TO BEING GRATEFUL TODAY ☐

Love cures people - both the ones who give it and the ones who receive it.

KARL MENNINGER

TODAY I AM GRATEFUL FOR

_____

_____

_____

_____

_____

_____

_____

_____

_____

MY INTENTION FOR TODAY IS

_____

_____

_____

ONE THING TO DO FOR MYSELF TODAY

_____

_____

WHAT CAN I DO TODAY TO FEEL

(Choose one.)

happy   /   healthy   /   kind   /   content   /   peaceful   /   patient   /   inspired

_____

_____

_____

THOUGHTS

I COMMIT TO BEING GRATEFUL TODAY ☐

In between goals is a thing called life that has to be lived and enjoyed.

SID CAESAR

TODAY I AM GRATEFUL FOR

_____

_____

_____

_____

_____

_____

_____

_____

_____

_____

MY INTENTION FOR TODAY IS

_____

_____

_____

ONE THING TO DO FOR MYSELF TODAY

_____

_____

WHAT CAN I DO TODAY TO FEEL

(Choose one.)

happy   /   healthy   /   kind   /   content   /   peaceful   /   patient   /   inspired

_____

_____

_____

THOUGHTS

True happiness... arises, in the first place, from the enjoyment of oneself, and in the next from the friendship and conversation of a few select companions.

JOSEPH ADDISON

TODAY I AM GRATEFUL FOR

MY INTENTION FOR TODAY IS

ONE THING TO DO FOR MYSELF TODAY

WHAT CAN I DO TODAY TO FEEL

(Choose one.)

happy / healthy / kind / content / peaceful / patient / inspired

THOUGHTS

Our lives are connected by a thousand invisible threads, and along these sympathetic fibers, our actions run as causes and return to us as results.

HERMAN MELVILLE

TODAY I AM GRATEFUL FOR

MY INTENTION FOR TODAY IS

ONE THING TO DO FOR MYSELF TODAY

WHAT CAN I DO TODAY TO FEEL

(Choose one.)

happy / healthy / kind / content / peaceful / patient / inspired

THOUGHTS

I COMMIT TO BEING GRATEFUL TODAY ☐

If anything is sacred the human body is sacred.

WALT WHITMAN

TODAY I AM GRATEFUL FOR

MY INTENTION FOR TODAY IS

ONE THING TO DO FOR MYSELF TODAY

WHAT CAN I DO TODAY TO FEEL

(Choose one.)

happy / healthy / kind / content / peaceful / patient / inspired

THOUGHTS

I COMMIT TO BEING GRATEFUL TODAY ☐

You control your destiny. You don't need magic to do it, and there are no magical shortcuts to solving your problems.

MERIDA, BRAVE

TODAY I AM GRATEFUL FOR

_____

_____

_____

_____

_____

_____

_____

_____

_____

_____

MY INTENTION FOR TODAY IS

_____

_____

_____

ONE THING TO DO FOR MYSELF TODAY

_____

_____

WHAT CAN I DO TODAY TO FEEL

(Choose one.)

happy   /   healthy   /   kind   /   content   /   peaceful   /   patient   /   inspired

_____

_____

_____

THOUGHTS

I COMMIT TO BEING GRATEFUL TODAY ☐

I know the price of success: dedication, hard work, and an unremitting devotion to the things you want to see happen.

FRANK LLOYD WRIGHT

TODAY I AM GRATEFUL FOR

MY INTENTION FOR TODAY IS

ONE THING TO DO FOR MYSELF TODAY

WHAT CAN I DO TODAY TO FEEL

(Choose one.)

happy / healthy / kind / content / peaceful / patient / inspired

THOUGHTS

I COMMIT TO BEING GRATEFUL TODAY ☐

You cannot dream yourself into a character.
You must hammer and forge yourself one.

JAMES A. FROUDE

TODAY I AM GRATEFUL FOR

_____

_____

_____

_____

_____

_____

_____

_____

_____

_____

_____

MY INTENTION FOR TODAY IS

_____

_____

_____

_____

ONE THING TO DO FOR MYSELF TODAY

_____

_____

WHAT CAN I DO TODAY TO FEEL

(Choose one.)

happy / healthy / kind / content / peaceful / patient / inspired

_____

_____

_____

_____

THOUGHTS

I COMMIT TO BEING GRATEFUL TODAY ☐

Following your feelings will lead you to their source. Only through emotions can you encounter the force field of your own soul.

GARY ZUKAV

TODAY I AM GRATEFUL FOR

MY INTENTION FOR TODAY IS

ONE THING TO DO FOR MYSELF TODAY

WHAT CAN I DO TODAY TO FEEL

(Choose one.)

happy / healthy / kind / content / peaceful / patient / inspired

THOUGHTS

I COMMIT TO BEING GRATEFUL TODAY ☐

/   /

*A successful marriage requires falling in love many times,
always with the same person.*

MIGNON MCLAUGHLIN

TODAY I AM GRATEFUL FOR

_____
_____
_____
_____
_____
_____
_____
_____
_____
_____
_____

MY INTENTION FOR TODAY IS

_____
_____
_____
_____

ONE THING TO DO FOR MYSELF TODAY

_____
_____

WHAT CAN I DO TODAY TO FEEL

(Choose one.)

happy   /   healthy   /   kind   /   content   /   peaceful   /   patient   /   inspired

_____
_____
_____
_____

THOUGHTS

I COMMIT TO BEING GRATEFUL TODAY ☐

Good friendships are fragile things and require as much care as any other fragile and precious thing.

RANDOLPH BOURNE

TODAY I AM GRATEFUL FOR

_____
_____
_____
_____
_____
_____
_____
_____
_____
_____

MY INTENTION FOR TODAY IS

_____
_____
_____

ONE THING TO DO FOR MYSELF TODAY

_____
_____

WHAT CAN I DO TODAY TO FEEL

(Choose one.)

happy / healthy / kind / content / peaceful / patient / inspired

_____
_____
_____

THOUGHTS

I COMMIT TO BEING GRATEFUL TODAY ☐

I don't seek. I find.

PABLO PICASSO

TODAY I AM GRATEFUL FOR

_____
_____
_____
_____
_____
_____
_____
_____
_____
_____
_____
_____

MY INTENTION FOR TODAY IS

_____
_____
_____
_____

ONE THING TO DO FOR MYSELF TODAY

_____
_____
_____

WHAT CAN I DO TODAY TO FEEL

(Choose one.)

happy / healthy / kind / content / peaceful / patient / inspired

_____
_____
_____
_____

THOUGHTS

Keeping your body healthy is an expression of gratitude to the whole cosmos –
The trees, the clouds, everything.

THICH NHAT HANH

TODAY I AM GRATEFUL FOR

_____

_____

_____

_____

_____

_____

_____

_____

_____

_____

_____

MY INTENTION FOR TODAY IS

_____

_____

_____

_____

ONE THING TO DO FOR MYSELF TODAY

_____

_____

_____

WHAT CAN I DO TODAY TO FEEL

(Choose one.)

happy / healthy / kind / content / peaceful / patient / inspired

_____

_____

_____

_____

THOUGHTS

I COMMIT TO BEING GRATEFUL TODAY ☐

Even miracles take a little time.

FAIRY GODMOTHER, CINDERELLA

TODAY I AM GRATEFUL FOR

_____

_____

_____

_____

_____

_____

_____

_____

_____

_____

_____

_____

MY INTENTION FOR TODAY IS

_____

_____

_____

_____

ONE THING TO DO FOR MYSELF TODAY

_____

_____

WHAT CAN I DO TODAY TO FEEL

(Choose one.)

happy   /   healthy   /   kind   /   content   /   peaceful   /   patient   /   inspired

_____

_____

_____

_____

THOUGHTS

I COMMIT TO BEING GRATEFUL TODAY ☐

/   /

Your work is to discover your world and then with all your heart give yourself to it.

BUDDHA

TODAY I AM GRATEFUL FOR

_____
_____
_____
_____
_____
_____
_____
_____
_____
_____
_____
_____

MY INTENTION FOR TODAY IS

_____
_____
_____
_____

ONE THING TO DO FOR MYSELF TODAY

_____
_____

WHAT CAN I DO TODAY TO FEEL

(Choose one.)

happy   /   healthy   /   kind   /   content   /   peaceful   /   patient   /   inspired

_____
_____
_____
_____

THOUGHTS

I COMMIT TO BEING GRATEFUL TODAY ☐

/ /

A person's character is their fate.

HERACLITUS

TODAY I AM GRATEFUL FOR

_____

_____

_____

_____

_____

_____

_____

_____

_____

_____

_____

MY INTENTION FOR TODAY IS

_____

_____

_____

ONE THING TO DO FOR MYSELF TODAY

_____

_____

WHAT CAN I DO TODAY TO FEEL

(Choose one.)

happy / healthy / kind / content / peaceful / patient / inspired

_____

_____

_____

_____

THOUGHTS

Bonus Section

Morning Joys!

Morning Joys are about investing the first 50 minutes of your day on *you* by doing three things you enjoy that empower your day to be a happy one.

No matter who you are and what you do, Morning Joys can change your life!

 HOW DO MORNING JOYS WORK?

Great question! They're super simple. All you do is choose three actions that:

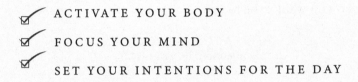

ACTIVATE YOUR BODY

FOCUS YOUR MIND

SET YOUR INTENTIONS FOR THE DAY

With consistency, you'll find that this simple routine will help you to become more positive and productive, calm and collected—all resulting in a happier you!

Let's begin!

 STEP #1 ACTIVATE YOUR BODY

Begin your morning with an easygoing 10-minute stretch routine. This could be yoga, pilates, or your favorite combo of simple stretches. The goal is to relax your mind and body awake.

WHAT YOU ACHIEVE
Muscles, stretched. Blood and oxygen, flowing. Body and mind, alert and energized.

 STEP #2 FOCUS YOUR MIND

You've enjoyed 10 minutes of stretching, and now it's time to meditate or journal for 20 minutes, which is a fantastic strategy to clear your mind. Whether you want to meditate for 10 minutes and journal for the rest or alternate days altogether, you've got options.

Trust your gut and remember that your Morning Joys will be as unique as you are!

WHAT YOU ACHIEVE
Body, calm. Mind, clear. Ability to be patient throughout the day, high.

☼ STEP #3 SET YOUR INTENTIONS FOR THE DAY

You've stretched, meditated and journaled. Now it's time to prioritize your goals and create a game plan for the day. (Aka, make your to-do list!).

This is where you decide not only what to do today but who to be today. Here are three thought-provoking prompts to help you get clear on who you want to be today:

Q: "My intention for today is..."

ex. Appreciate the little things.

Q: "I want to practice feeling..."

ex. Healthy, happy and kind.

Q: "I will treat myself and others with..."

ex. Patience, kindness and respect.

WHAT YOU ACHIEVE
A clear, concise decision on how you'll treat yourself and others throughout the day. (Talk about being intentional!)

FAQ

WHEN IS THE BEST TIME TO DO MY MORNING JOYS?

The best time to do your Morning Joys is **an hour before** you get ready for the day.

The goal is to start your day with ease and enjoy these quiet, private moments, so schedule a time that you can commit to daily.

WHAT IF MY LITTLE ONE WAKES UP WHILE I'M IN THE MIDDLE OF DOING MY MORNING JOYS?

Fabulous question! Got a great support system at home? *(Mine is my hubby)*. Ask them to support you by taking care of your little one if they wake up during your Morning Joys.

Welcome your little sweetie into what you're doing. This may mean modifying your stretch routine into more of a quiet cuddle session, and that's cool. Cuddle sessions bring joy, too!

option 2

I'M ALL ABOUT THAT HEALTHY LIFE. WHEN SHOULD I WORKOUT?

If you've got a busy day, schedule your work-out to immediately follow your Morning Joys.

This is what personally works for me, so I wake up 90 minutes before my two little boys instead of an hour.

WHERE CAN I FIND FREE MEDITATION MUSIC?

YouTube is a great go-to source. Check out the Meditative Mind channel. Its' guided meditations will help during mornings when you feel distracted.

I'VE TRIED MEDITATION BEFORE AND FOUND IT SUPER HARD. ANY SUGGESTIONS?

It can feel hard when first starting, but that's no reason not to do it!

So my #1 suggestion is **try it again**. Today, tomorrow, and so on.

Consistency is your best friend when it comes to meditation, so stay at it and be kind to yourself. Focus on progress, not perfection. I promise it will soon become second nature to you.

You may also want to consider Transcendental Meditation, which I found to be the easiest way to learn meditation. It's what I use today and let me tell ya, it's as easy as breathing!

HOW DO I PRIORITIZE MY TO-DO LIST?

Let's start with what you don't do.

You don't make other people's to-do list yours. No matter how much of an emergency they make their request seem, or how tempted you feel to give in and say, *"Yeah, I'll do it."*

Contrary to popular belief, it's okay to kindly say, *"No."*

So when that request pops up, ask yourself:

1. *How easily would this fit into my schedule?*
2. *Does this help me achieve my goals for the day?*
3. *Do I even want to do this?*

Depending on your answers, you may want to respond with: *"I wish I could help out, but it won't be possible for me today. I hope you can figure out another way to get that done."*

Rarely is it easy to say, *"No."* so say the above lines out loud a few times until you feel comfortable with them, and be courageous enough to kindly decline.

So, back to prioritizing your to-do list ... mentally sift through what you think you *"have to"* do today.

For each task, ask yourself these three questions:

- ☐ Do I have to do this? Or can someone else easily do this for me? (ex. cleaning the house, grocery shopping, laundry, etc.)

- ☐ If this one thing was all I did today, would I feel accomplished?

- ☐ Does this have to be done today?

If the answer is *"No,"* then save that to-do for another day.

Congrats!

YOU JUST LEARNED HOW TO:

- ☐ Wake up with the routine to have a more positive and productive day.

- ☐ Start (and continue) enjoyable and effective habits.

- ☐ Use the power of positivity and proven practices to create health in your mind and body.

Check the boxes when you're done!